ART AS A BRIDGE BETWEEN THE SENSIBLE AND THE SUPERSENSIBLE

THE SOCIAL QUESTION

Rudolf Steiner

From Rudolf Steiner: *Vergangenheits- und Zukunftsimpulse im sozialen Geschehen*
(Past and Future Impulses in Social Life)
GA 190, Lecture VI, 30th March 1919

Translated by Peter Stebbing

First Printing
Copyright © October 2021
The e.Lib, Inc.
Anthroposophical Publications
https://AnthroposophicalPublications.org/

This is the sixth in a series of twelve lectures given by _Rudolf Steiner,_ contained in the volume _Vergangenheits- und Zukunftsimpulse im sozialen Geschehen_ (Past and Future Impulses in Social Life). GA 190. The heading of this single lecture derives from the translator.

Cover Design by Peter Stebbing.
The graphic form reproduces an original pencil sketch of Rudolf Steiner from a notebook of September 1920.
"Anthros" lettering by Peter Zeswitsch.
Initial letter "W" on p. 1, by Rudolf Steiner.

Lecture translated by Peter Stebbing

Editing by James D. Stewart
Emeritus e.Librarian at the
The e.Lib, Inc.
https://www.elib.com/

Printed in the United States of America

Paperback: ISBN 978-1-948302-22-7
Kindle: ISBN 978-1-948302-23-4
On-line: ISBN 978-1-948302-24-1

The human being can accomplish what he should accomplish; and if he says he cannot, he does not want to.

Johann Gottlieb Fichte

Art As A Bridge Between The Sensible And The Supersensible

The Social Question

Rudolf Steiner

Lecture of 30th March 1919

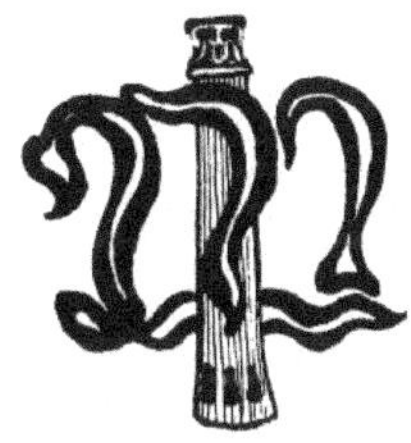

HAT is called the social question asserts itself in the most decisive manner in our time, as a historic challenge. However, at the same time, it has to be said: Our present age is little prepared to approach the social question in its true form with active comprehension. On this point one has only to avoid yielding to illusions. We have often had to indicate the profound chasm existing in our time between the leading classes and social ranks and the proletarian masses. In the course of recent historical developments, the leading classes and social ranks have allied themselves with certain interest groups and have neglected to cultivate a generally human understanding. The proletarian masses have increasingly had to regard themselves as excluded by virtue of their entire life situation from what the leading classes have essentially concocted for themselves. As regards the division into classes, the situation in ancient Greece, for example, could be said to have been still more unfavorable. At that time there was the large number of slaves who not only partially, with regard to their capacity for work, but with respect to their entire humanity, were viewed as a commodity to be bought and sold on the open market. Yet it would be wrong even so to see it as a matter of looking at this alone. Well into modern times a sharp class distinction and class division has certainly persisted, though it has existed more in terms of the external aspects of life, as expressed in one's social status.

More recently — and precisely this is of significance — a kind of cultural commonality closely connected to the egoistic interests of these leading classes has spread far and wide — in which the great proletarian masses are unable to participate. One need really only consider how little the cultural life of earlier ages assumed this direction. In ancient times there were single individuals to be sure, Mystery leaders, students of the Mysteries imbued with the higher elements of spiritual life, but this spiritual life did not take the form it does today — such that the human being undergoes a bourgeois education, donning superior civic garb as compared to the worker's overalls, while relegating the worker to only a proletarian education. One need but think of how Christianity endeavored for centuries to imbue humanity with a common spiritual life, aiming to represent all human beings as equal before God. In the same way, if you look back for that matter to the cultural life of the ancient Hebrews, there were of course the scribes and Pharisees, single communities that stood out, that were in possession of a certain spiritual life, but what they gave out of this spiritual life, they gave in the same way to all classes of people. Class division concerned other matters than cultural life itself. And it should not be forgotten that throughout the Middle Ages the content of spiritual life lay in something quite different than it does today. The content of spiritual life in the Middle Ages resided in the images to be found in the church, where everyone could see them, where the highest nobility could see them, where the last of the poor could see them. Spiritual life united people from above and below.

Then came more recent times that essentially replaced the old pictorial element with what is literary. Ever less understanding showed itself for the pictorial, for what is of an imaginative nature. More and more, people sought educational development by means of literature, by means of the written and printed word. And this written and printed word increasingly took on the form that made it possible to a certain extent that, alongside the proletarian, universally-human feeling, an upper stratum emerged in education. This soul-duality in social life has manifested itself ever more in recent times and has laid the basis, more than anything else, for the profound social chasm that now has such frightful consequences.

In addition, it transpired that in this fifth post-Atlantean time-period involving the development of the consciousness soul, human beings became more and more egoistic. In a sense, a pinnacle had to be attained in evolving the human personality. By virtue of this development of the human personality, human beings became less and less capable of understanding each other in reality, of entering into each other. We have finally arrived in this present age at the point where it has become almost impossible for one person to be convinced of another. On that account, spreading ideas is so easily sought on the path of violence. How often have I not emphasized here and elsewhere in our Society, that nowadays, on the basis of no prerequisites of any kind, everyone actually has his standpoint. Today someone can be a presumptuous young whippersnapper and still have his standpoint with regard to even the most mature way of thinking. The feeling that a point of view for judging life is to be won by way of maturation, by way of extended experience, this sense has reached the point of disappearing altogether. Entering into the other person, becoming convinced of what lives in the soul of the other person — this has retreated more and more. Hence people understand each other so little — indeed to an ever-diminishing extent.

Further, in the course of the last centuries human beings have turned away more and more from spirituality. I recently emphasized here once again that one should not deceive oneself in that people still go to church, maintaining they have religion. This "religion" signifies extraordinarily little as compared with the connection the human being needs and ought to seek, between the sense world in which he lives between birth and death, and the supersensible world. The greater part of what people claim for themselves today as religious content is after all nothing more than a living in words, a living in language. And having stressed yesterday and the day-before-yesterday, how abstract this life in language has become, it need not surprise us that religious life, expressing itself for the most part for people in language, has become abstract and hence materialistic. For, everything abstract leads human beings continuously to what is materialistic. And the question that should in fact imbue us inwardly and resonate throughout our entire life: "What is the human being in reality?" is one that points to something barely approached by the average person today. I ask you to consider, after all, that in order to answer the question, "What is the human being?" one needs, in a devoted manner, to enter into the whole world; for the human being is a microcosm, a little world, and only becomes comprehensible if conceived of as born out of the entire world. Understanding the human being presupposes understanding the world. Yet, how little is a real understanding of the world actually sought (and hence a real understanding of the human being) in a natural scientific age that enters purely into what is external. If nowadays such considerations are deemed to have nothing to do with understanding the social question, it nonetheless remains true that everything I have set forth here is intimately connected with understanding the social question. This will only gradually be acknowledged once again in reaching the point of wanting to enter lovingly into what is spiritual. Today, the intention is solely to solve the social question on the basis of externalities. It will only really be solved, however, in seeing spiritual experience as the basis of all human striving, feeling and willing — in being able to pose the question once again: How can a true relationship be established between the world in which the human being lives between birth and death, and the world in which he lives between death and a new birth?

You will already be more or less familiar with the "Group Statue" which is to depict the trinity for the worldview of the future: "The Representative of Humanity between Lucifer and Ahriman." You may have become aware that the attempt is to depict this Representative of Humanity in a way that otherwise corresponds only to the human countenance with its features.

The human countenance with its features is an expression of the soul-life. With respect to the human being, we speak of physiognomy, of certain external gestures, and we recognize this mobility expressing itself in physiognomy and gesture as being connected to the soul life. In the Representative of Humanity of our group statue the aim was not only to portray the countenance in so far as it assumes a physiognomic expression in the human being between birth and death. The further attempt was, as it were, to portray the human being as a whole according to the principle by which nature builds up the human countenance — making every formation, every limb, so to speak, an extension of the countenance. Why something like this? Because in our time the endeavor has to take hold once more of calling forth a common understanding between beings that live only as soul-spiritual beings, and beings that live here on the earth in human physical bodies. Let us remind ourselves as before, of what the dead learn of our language — what they perceive, in so far as they perceive anything of our earth.

On the earth we first of all have the mineral kingdom. We have this mineral kingdom to a certain extent in the form of crystals, and we have broken-up, amorphous minerals as they are called. Basically, of the earth element the dead see only crystal forms and those of the earth's formations that result in regular figures, seeing them as empty voids. You can read about these things in my *Theosophy*. Of the plants the dead do not see in the first place the forms we see with our eyes. It is actually rather difficult to point to what the dead see of the plant world. For them, the whole of the earth's plant world is like a vast body, but they do not see the green plant forms that we see, only a certain movement, the growth process of the plants. They see precisely what escapes the human being. They see the earth as a great unified organism and the "hair" so to speak, growing spiritually out of the earth — for the plants are spiritualized. Again, of the animal world — I am referring to the outer sensible forms — the dead see only the running of the animals over the earth, not the individual forms of the animals, but their spatial alteration.

And, in as much as they can be accounted physical forms, what do the dead see of human beings? Well, the dead see nothing at all of human beings, with the exception of just a few parts. They perceive the soul, the spiritual, but the outer form not at all. Thus if we were to form the Representative of Humanity as a human figure appears on the earth, this figure would be quite imperceptible for the dead, as also for the Angeloi and Archangeloi. For all beings no longer possessing a body in which there are physical eyes, the human figure, portrayed purely according to its physical form is something invisible, something imperceptible. And only if you begin to express the soul element in the form, so that the external form does not correspond to the human form naturalistically in the here and now, only then do the dead begin to see the form. If you look at a normal, symmetrical face — as faces generally are not, but how people see them — of such a so-called work of art the dead see nothing at all. Our sculptural figure could only be made visible also for supersensible beings in being asymmetrical, in especially emphasizing asymmetry, that is, in containing something of a soul nature that otherwise does not come to expression naturalistically in the external form.

But call to mind how art has become increasingly naturalistic in recent times. Perhaps I already related that I once knew a young person, a sculptor, who had even acquired a name for himself in his native country, who said — we were talking about artistic monuments — to my horror: "Well, the finest rendering of a human being would result from copying every detail of the person precisely, in stone or in bronze, or in some other material." I replied, "That would be as far removed as it possibly could be from a work of art!" For in reality, a work of art should have nothing in common with such a mere reproduction. It should be anything but like the original. He could not understand that. A "casting" actually counted for him as the most perfect work of sculpture. But it could be said, much of recent art is formed on the basis of this way of thinking, as well as prevailing opinions on art. Whence, ultimately, is any other opinion on art to be derived? After all, on seeing a statue in marble or bronze or in another material, people have to experience something or other! And if they have no relation at all to a spiritual world, they can hardly come to any other judgment than in asking themselves, "Is that in accordance with nature, is there something like that in nature?" And if someone finds that nothing of the sort exists in nature, he then considers what art portrays as having no justification.

But, my dear friends, let us remind ourselves again and again, that it is actually quite absurd to replicate life naturalistically! To write dramas in the manner of *Gerhart Hauptmann* (1862-1946) is ridiculous, since that can self-evidently, be done better in real life. In this respect, we cannot keep up with nature, after all. Whatever is gained from the spiritual world, on the other hand, is a valuable addition to nature. It represents something new placed into this world. But recent times have turned ever more to naturalism, amounting to materialism on a historical level. [It should perhaps be noted that, in her recollections, Margarita Woloschin reports, "Once, after visiting an exhibition of modern art, Dr. Steiner said, 'Non-representational painting is a protest against naturalism, but strictly speaking it is absurd.'" *Transl.*]

All this stems from human beings turning away from spiritual life. A sound return to spiritual life is only possible in conceiving the relation of the sensible to the supersensible in concrete terms, such as we have now attempted to do in various fields, making clear to ourselves what the dead hears of speech and sees in the way of forms that exist for the earthly human being. If we make concretely clear to ourselves, in detail, what the relationships are for the sensible and supersensible, in the same way we do for something on the physical plane, then only do we gain a real idea of the connection between the sensible and supersensible! The emerging materialistic naturalism of recent times that has taken hold of people ever more forcefully since the 15th, 16th century has killed the sense for this connection of the sensible and supersensible. Finally, natural science lets nothing count as valid other than sensible reality. In this manner, human beings have torn themselves away from a true, living, feeling-connection with the spiritual world.

In separate branches of civilization in the 18th century this took yet another turn. Within French culture, among the Encyclopedists (1751-80) [identified with the rationalism of the Enlightenment], materialism yielded its ingenious results. This spread far and wide. And finally there came what leads most of all away from the spiritual world: the life in theosophical abstractions! This life in theosophical abstractions limits itself to saying, the human being consists of physical body, ether body, astral body and so on; the human being has a karma, the human being lives in repeated earth lives. It wants to teach these abstractions as something grandiose, while remaining stuck in words, leading in the end to the extreme arrogance prevalent in many theosophical societies. There one remains completely in words, in externalities. Only in passing over to questions such as, "What do the dead hear of what we say? What do the dead see of what we have here in our surroundings?", only in proceeding to such concrete ideas do real thoughts reveal themselves concerning the spiritual world. The utmost extremes border on each other: empty words and blather such as "astral body", "ether body" and so on, behind which there is often nothing at all but words and pure naturalistic materialism.

It is absolutely necessary to acquire a feeling for these things, a feeling such that one demands to hear in concrete terms about the relationship of the physical and supra-physical world. And only in permeating ourselves with such definite ideas of the connection between the physical and the supra-physical world can we return once again to what in a different manner human beings of older epochs possessed — return, that is, to more wide-ranging world-interests. We can ask, why has so much misfortune broken out over the world? Well, the ultimate reason is that people's interests have become so narrow as to barely transcend the most everyday matters. Naturally, if the human being ceases to interest himself in the stars, he then begins to interest himself in kaffeeklatsch. If the human being ceases to survey the relation of the higher hierarchies in his own thoughts, the inclination arises in him to waste time in ordinary dilly-dallying. It is only necessary to look at what interests have occupied the leading circles of humanity over the last centuries. One need only take account of what these people do from morning to evening! And if one does so with comprehension, one will not be surprised that such a debacle has befallen humanity. Nowadays people are glad if they can gain a rough idea of something in just a few words! They are pleased if they can encompass this or that without any effort.

The historical development of humanity speaks in clear terms of the various possibilities for viewing things. There are countless examples in this respect. In recent years, for instance, German culture has frequently been reproached for having a *Hegel* [Georg Wilhelm Friedrich Hegel, 1770-1831] with his theory of the state, i.e., for Hegel having said, the state in the end is something like a kind of god on earth. But it should be remembered that German culture had not only Hegel, but *Stirner* [Max Stirner, 1806-56], not separated by many years at all from Hegel. While for Hegel the state was something like an ever-changing earth-god, for Stirner the state was worthless trash, something to be negated. The two lived in close proximity to each other. One can hardly imagine two greater extremes arising from the same cultural life. If one then wants to portray such a cultural life, then one has to do so as I did in my *Riddles of Philosophy*, for example, where the one thinker is accorded the same weight as the other. On first reading about Hegel, you might be led to believe I adhered to Hegel's viewpoint. Then, in reading about Stirner, you might assume I adhered to Stirner's viewpoint. With that, nothing else is implied than that we should train ourselves to acquire understanding for the many-sidedness of human beings, and gain inner tolerance. It should interest us, what is conceived by another soul quite differently than what we ourselves have thought. For we should have the feeling, this other thought complements our own.

Let us say there are a number of people, ten individuals (a sketch was made), I am one of them, the other nine are there. I now say to myself, I think about certain matters in one way, the second person in another way, the third again differently, and so on, all varying in some degree. All are right, none are right. If we sense the approximate arithmetical middle of all this, if in this context we feel able to take up everything with the same love, irrespective of whether we say it, or others say it, learning to feel ourselves within the totality, then we join in hastening toward the purpose that exists for the human beings of the future. We must strive for this "hastening." We must strive for it simply in order to gain a feeling for true social life. We must learn to feel ourselves standing within what is comprised by the genius of language, by what is comprised by the life of rights, by the rights-genius. We must learn to stand within what is encompassed by the mutually shared economic genius. Only this living feeling of being within a totality that has to be consciously acquired in the age of the consciousness-soul — only this propels the human being toward humanity's future destination. However, we cannot attain this approach to the human being's future destination in any other way than by extending our interests ever further, in other words, in learning to overcome ourselves more and more. Yes, my dear friends, in taking counsel with oneself quite honestly, one will after all find in the end, that actually what is of least interest in the whole world is what one is able to think and feel about oneself within the narrow confines of the "I." Indeed, in our age many people occupy their thoughts and feelings to a great extent within the most immediate boundaries of their "I." Hence their life is so boring and hence they are so dissatisfied with life. We never become interesting in always only circling around this midpoint. In contrast to this, if we look out, always focusing on how the external world shines toward us, if we expand our interests ever farther, then our "I" becomes interesting by virtue of giving us a standpoint for observing the world. Then our "I" becomes significant through the fact that, just from this point of the "I," only we are capable of seeing the world, as no other person can. Another person sees it from a different standpoint.

However, if we remain within ourselves, circling continuously around our own self, we contemplate in fact only what we have in common with all other people. And then, in the end every other person loses interest for us — and ultimately the whole world actually loses interest for us. A widening of interest is above all what is striven for by means of spiritual science. However, in order to experience this widening of interest it is necessary for us to educate ourselves to become receptive for what approaches us from outside, so that we really can take up something new. People do not reject spiritual science because it is difficult — it is not actually difficult — they repudiate it for the reason that it does not roll on in the well-worn trains of thought they are used to, since it requires them to engage in new trains of thought. People reject everything that calls for new trains of thought. One can encounter quite peculiar things in this respect. The content of the *"Aufruf"* [The March 1919 "Appeal to the German People and the Cultural World" contained in GA 23 and GA 189] which will be known to you, as also various things on the social question contained in the paper that is to appear in a few days' time, I communicated to certain personalities during the last horrifying years. It would really have been a question of these people learning from bitter experience to act of themselves as necessity demanded. In speaking to one or another individual of the need for cultural life to be placed on an independent footing, and not continue to be combined with the state and economic spheres, people listened. On many such occasions, it initially appeared as though they exerted themselves to arrive at a thought in this connection. In one's presence, while speaking, people are polite and do not conduct themselves as when they are only supposed to read something. Having thus given the matter a thought, the gesture of politeness (which has no truth to it) is over — and then the "thought machine" shuts off again, and one heard the same thing every time, "Oh yes, the separation of church and school is comprehensible!" That was the only thing they had actually heard, the one thing that has been said over and over again in one way or another for generations — well-worn trains of thought. The rest dissolves like sound and smoke.

Here we touch on things that need to change in our time. We should cultivate the devoted attitude that leads to receptivity for revelations that, as I mentioned here a while ago, would reveal themselves in our time to human beings from the spiritual world. How often, of late, one heard the words, "Simple, everything has to be simple!" The most sensible, the brightest people could be heard quoting Goethe, saying for instance, "The all-comprehending One, does He not comprehend you, me, Himself?" "A name is sound and smoke, feeling is everything" — and so on. It was all supposed to be very profound. But Goethe wrote this as Faust's instruction to a sixteen-year-old girl. That was forgotten! What was well suited to the heartstrings of the naïve Gretchen became profound philosophical wisdom! People do not notice such things. But it is easier, self-evidently, to understand what is appropriate for the sixteen-year-old Gretchen, than what is not appropriate for a sixteen-year-old Gretchen, but for mature human beings. In our time, people should take account of such aberrations and break with all too many inherited notions. Reverberating through modern culture there has also been what contains seeds for the future. A while ago I quoted here a saying of *Fichte* [Johann Gottlieb Fichte, 1762-1814], "The human being can accomplish what he should accomplish; and if he says, he cannot, he does not want to." This is a most important saying, one the modern human being needs above all as a guideline. This is because the modern human being is not permitted to be a layabout, saying in regard to certain things, "I can't do that." It lies in the nature of the modern human being that he can do far more than he often supposes, and that "genius" has to be for him more and more a result of diligence. However, one has to be capable of gaining belief in this diligence for oneself. As far as possible one has to rid oneself of every thought that one would be unable to do whatever it is one ought to do. It should constantly be kept in mind just how easy it is to claim that one would be incapable of doing something, merely because making the attempt would be uncongenial. And the more the modern human being makes this an everyday rule, the more will he attain the mood of the soul-spiritual. In more people than you might think, this mood will call forth the inner experience of what anthroposophically oriented spiritual science wants to say. What anthroposophical spiritual science wants to say is available, my dear friends, at least in regard to certain elementary matters. It is available for the human soul. One need only summon the courage to have it. In developing the corresponding mood, the social understanding and the social interest will develop. For when do we have no social understanding? We have no social understanding only when we have no interests that transcend our immediate concerns. Social understanding awakens at once when we take an interest in what lies beyond our immediate circle; albeit really and truly! Taking these things into consideration is quite especially necessary in the age of the evolving consciousness soul. It is necessary for the reason that in the age of the consciousness soul the cosmic powers point the human being to the "I". Hence, the human being has to be all the more vigilant in transcending the "I"! Since so many antisocial forces rise up from the depths of the human soul today, the social element has to be consciously cultivated that we send down once again into subconscious depths. Most people today do not really know what to do with themselves. But that comes from only wanting to occupy oneself with one's own concerns. The moment we do not merely occupy ourselves with personal matters, but enter into a feeling relation to the whole world, then we begin to do what is right for ourselves.

These things are closely allied to understanding the social question. In many respects the social question is a soul question. But only someone standing within anthroposophical spiritual science will know to sense it rightly as a soul question. That is what I wanted to say to you today.

(Translated by Peter Stebbing, January 2021)

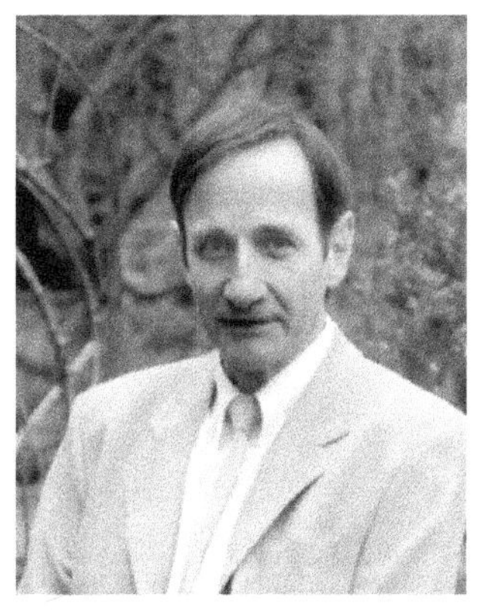

Born in Copenhagen, Denmark in 1941, Peter Stebbing attended Waldorf Schools in England. Having studied at art schools in Brighton and London, he emigrated to the United States in 1966, continuing his studies at Cornell University and earning the M.F.A. degree in painting in 1968.

While teaching design and colour courses over a period of six years in the City University of New York, he began a practical exploration of the scientific colour phenomena set forth by Goethe in his colour theory. This led eventually to a turning point – to the crucial question of finding a corresponding approach to colour in painting.

The new and wholly different training in colour experience begun in 1976 with the painter Gerard Wagner on the basis of Rudolf Steiner's motif sketches, resolved fundamental artistic questions with a coherent and systematic approach. Fully in accord with Goethe's discoveries and method, this approach may be termed "Goetheanistic."

Peter Stebbing subsequently established a painting school at the Threefold Educational Foundation in Spring Valley, N.Y., teaching there from 1983 until 1990. Since 1992 he has been director of the Arteum Painting School (http://www.arteum-malschule.de/) in Dornach, Switzerland. He is also the translator and editor of various anthroposophical art publications.

BOOKS TRANSLATED AND EDITED
BY PETER STEBBING

- Margarita Woloschin, *The Green Snake. An Autobiography*. Floris Books, 2010. 431 pages paperback.

- Elisabeth Wagner-Koch and Gerard Wagner, *The Individuality of Colour. Contributions to a Methodical Schooling in Colour Experience*. 2nd edition. 128 pages. Hardcover. Rudolf Steiner Press, 2009.

- *The Goetheanum Cupola Motifs of Rudolf Steiner. Paintings by Gerard Wagner*. 236 pages. Hardcover. SteinerBooks, 2011.

- *Conversations about Painting with Rudolf Steiner. Recollections of Five Pioneers of the New Art Impulse*. 195 pages, 77 illustrations, hardcover. SteinerBooks, 2008.

- *Three Grimms' Fairy Tales. Paintings by Gerard Wagner*. 70 pages with 31 colour plates, hardcover. SteinerBooks, 2012.

- Rudolf Steiner, *The World of Fairy Tales*. 23 black-and-white shaded drawings by Gerard Wagner. 124 pages, paperback, Kindle. SteinerBooks 2013.

- *The Art of Colour and the Human Form: Seven Motif Sketches of Rudolf Steiner: Studies by Gerard Wagner*. 218 pages, hardcover. Verlag des Ita Wegman Instituts, 2017. Also available from SteinerBooks, Great Barrington, USA.

- _Fairy Tales: in the Light of Spiritual Investigation_. 56 pages, paperback, Kindle, on-line. Rudolf Steiner Publications, 2019.

- _Leonardo's Spiritual Stature: at the Turning Point of Modern Times_. 40 pages, paperback, Kindle, on-line. Rudolf Steiner Publications, 2019.

- _Raphael's Mission: in the Light of the Science of the Spirit_. 44 pages, paperback, Kindle, on-line. Rudolf Steiner Publications, 2018.

- _The Worldview of Herman Grimm: In Relation to Spiritual Science_. 52 pages, paperback, Kindle, on-line. Rudolf Steiner Publications, 2019.

ON-LINE ACTIVITIES

- On-line *Search* of Bn/GA# 190 texts
- On-line *Compare* of Bn/GA# 190 texts
- Rudolf Steiner Archive & e.Lib: Bn/GA# 190 <u>Overview page</u>
- Wikipedia: <u>Rudolf Steiner</u>

www.ingramcontent.com/pod-product-compliance
Lightning Source LLC
Chambersburg PA
CBHW070829260726

48654CB00024B/659